Cry Baby

Gareth Writer-Davies

Indigo Dreams Publishing

First Edition: Cry Baby
First published in Great Britain in 2017 by:
Indigo Dreams Publishing Ltd
24 Forest Houses
Halwill
Beaworthy
EX21 5UU
www.indigodreams.co.uk

Gareth Writer-Davies has asserted his right under the
Copyright, Designs and Patents Act 1988 to be identified as the
author of this work.
©2017 Gareth Writer-Davies

ISBN 978-1-910834-51-0

British Library Cataloguing in Publication Data. A CIP record
for this book can be obtained from the British Library.

Designed and typeset in Palatino Linotype by Indigo Dreams.
Author photograph by Jade Findlater at
https://www.flickr.com/photos/jadefindlater/
Cover design by Ronnie Goodyer at Indigo Dreams
Printed and bound in Great Britain by: 4edge Ltd
www.4edge.co.uk

Papers used by Indigo Dreams are recyclable products made from
wood grown in sustainable forests following the guidance of the
Forest Stewardship Council.

Thanks go to the following publications in which some of the poems originally featured:

Black Sheep Journal, Carillon, The Screech Owl, Sarasvati, Ink, Sweat and Tears, San Pedro River Review (USA), Monkey Kettle, Prole, Poetry Bay (USA) The British Edition, Brain of Forgetting.

To Poetry ID for their inspiration and commitment, to Ira Lightman whose maxims made a difference and to my sisters for their pre-reading of this collection.

Thank you to David Van Cauter for his excellent editorial advice.

Also by Gareth Writer-Davies

Bodies

CONTENTS

Cry Baby

I was made
in a black iron bed

swaddled in a feather quilt
nylon slick
and fuchsia pink

that had I focus
would have foretold

hunter of foxes
cornet in a military band
designer of frocks

I was not the imagined girl
ready for gingham ribbons and ankle socks

I was something else

with a purple scream
a fist of a child
who bit my mother's breast
and kicked out at rainbows

Love
after Toon Tellegen

after he gave up innocence
(believing her a maid)

my father
did not want to love my mother

so he gave her children

but that
was not enough

he wanted badly
to not love her

so gave her nothing
but soap
whiter than snow

what more
he did not know

so he gave her melancholia
and tradition

and that was how
he did not love her

Battleships

the enigmatic grid
on which the first guess is a shot in the dark

but a good memory
a notepad
and you can build up an image

of the enemy at anchor
waiting to return fire

when broken
the code scatters to the horizon at a speed of thirty two knots

the cautionary wreckage of the mother ship
a hazard to navigation

the game of imagination
that taught me all I need to know about explosives

The Childish Bed

when
on long sunburn holidays

we would be put to bed
naked
smothered in Savlon

and tell knuckle rude stories
barely laughing

in the morning
cuddled up and snoring

our parents
woke us shouting

when we
are within the touch tender shape

is love
anything more than bare sentiment

arousal
that stirs us into action

back to the time when tired but true
our hot flesh was all innocence

Milko

humming
the milk van delivered

dairy goods
for breakfast and pud

like a carnival float
the bouncing cargo

of gold and silver tops
danced in the crate

with one pint-ers
that bumped along the dark garden path

jumping
the sleepy traffic lights

Fred the milkman
is dead

Rover

there was a time when a Rover
meant that you roved

and a Singer sang a merry song
as you motored
down country lanes

getting from A to B
and back to A
was an adventure

topping up the radiator
(every stop)
the rust was unbelievable

but complaint
is churlish

back then
a gallon
the challenge of the frugal spark

took you to places
that you couldn't have imagined

The Train Is Coming

I shouted
the train is coming

a toddler on his first trip
to London
beyond reason on a rainy day

the doors whispered
and we were on our way

we chatted and pointed
imagined the phantoms of the dark

but my parent's inabilities
were clear
as we bumped along the track

and when the little train stopped for breath
I came up for air
in Kentish Town
alone and inexact

my parents
two hundred feet below
lost in the puzzle of the map

I cried
as though
my heart were broken

The Bank Manager

my father
never brought his work home
(which was a shame)

1/ turn the locks

2/steady the wobbly chair

3/ hide sharp objects

4/ check the medicine cabinet

then he could relax
and eat his dinner

once my father had hoped to be a hard-boiled crime writer
then found he had nothing to say

so put his temper
into managing my mother

Tonguesmith

my father
had a shameless mouth

sharp to the word, quick to the action
handsome

he never missed a chance
to stick his tongue, where it wasn't wanted

to return a quip
doubled, with a little extra acid

women thought him dashing

a tonguesmith
sans pareil

whose strong words
were a shield

whose fiery lips
could talk them into anything

the tongue
slick like a snake

busy
like a blade

and lips twice bitten
are shy
like a child's heart, broken

my father
only wanted a bit of fun

this won him
many admirers but few friends

his tongue
both a curse and a blessing

a kiss can be forgiven
but words
can never be unspoken

so
they are written

Marilyn

I was a platinum blonde

with curls
and a firm grip on my fortitude

I went to school
wearing my sister's dress

I liked being a girl
never doubted, I would be a star of stage and screen

but when my roots
began to show through

I was put in shorts
and elasticated socks

that
is how I have remained

Child

the house has become an organism
watching and feeding
turning

there is a smudge of something
an indent of the air

I have grown used to the idea
and set a trap
using the window as a mirror

I am startled
by my own silhouette

tomorrow
I shall renew my acquaintance

lie beneath the feathered quilt
and wait

Elocution

to lengtheeen
our vowelS

learn how to acT
an(d) not forgeT
wheRe wee Came frrrom

lessonssss
thaT have staaayed wiTH meee
despiTe my BesT INtentionnns

Mother came frrrom a TerraceD hous(e)
iN the hearT
of an inDustrrrial wasTeland

an(d) Never looked BacK

Wood Pigeons

our neighbours
were the first in the street
to have two cars

but the houses were built
when one car
was quite an achievement

so they took down the hawthorn trees
in which bloody wood pigeons
nested amongst the blossom

and with an excavator
widened
their side of the drive

outraged
my mother dug three holes
to hold fast growing conifers

that gave up their leaves
on every day of the year
and oozed acid

the gregarious wood pigeons
moved on
the turtle doves too

leaving us
down the pecking order

our neighbours
were the first in the street
to have a television

and that
was unforgiveable

Piano Lessons

the conservatory, was built on dirt
so the damp
ran straight up the walls

I practised my scales
made multichromatic by the warp
of the hammers and strings

if I hit a G
a G#
hung in the cool nascent air

my piano teacher
closing one eye
would bend his finger, touch his lips

the metronome, seeking perfect time
soon
we understood each other

Swimming At Aberdovey

my mother, had never forgiven my father
for being attractive to other women

so she made up her mind
to swim across the estuary to Ynyslas

midstream, between one shore and the other
she was picked up

by a rowdy boat of fishermen
who joked
that they had caught a mermaid

and brought her back to the beach
to the family she had not thought to see again

Elephant

I was a fat kid
who moved unwell on land

so, I woke up with the birds
and shuffled slowly, to the municipal pool

with the water all to myself
I floated, in my blubber suit

my snorkel
like an elephant's trunk

the weight of the world
was held by the surface tension

then with a giant splash
I flipped

and watched the barm of bubbles
race into the turquoise
of the deep

Tennis With Virginia
after John Betjeman

my strength lay in the advantage court
where all summer long
I thumped backhand drives

and sliced the kicking serve
to give you
easy put away volleys

how sweet it would have been
to stroke a forehand winner
from your side of the court

the stirring coda to a dramatic game, set and match
of mixed doubles

when short in sleeve and strong in shorts
we knew
each others game

Lilac Ladies

mother was a virgin
when on Boxing Day she married

this came out, when my sister was thrown out
for having sex with her boyfriend

moved
by the violation of her hearth and home

she slammed, the door so hard
that the fanlight buckled

the drowsy wallpaper
woke up
and the lovely lilac ladies

agreed that it was all for the best

Pyjamas

nobody else wanted the house

it came with a tenant
the abandoned wife

who chased me from room to room

once I saw a yellowhammer
and confusing it for a tennis ball

hammered it for six
over long cover

in the laundry room
my mother kept geraniums

sometimes
there was a knock on the door

then I'd dream
I was walking the streets in my pyjamas

Coracles

after my father
had slipped the farmer a bob

I sat midstream
an inch or two above the deep fish pools of the River Teifi
as ticked sheep were bellowed from one county to the other

we ducked the reluctant ewes
with the long paddle
and watched the field bugs float away

I was happy
impressed that my father spoke to the farmer in his native tongue

and did not think that sheep could drown
as we carved upon the waters and skewed under the bridge
our nutshell boats

my father bought the grieving farmer a pint and a whiskey
to chase it down
and agreed that the boy was a Jonah

Grand Union Canal

where one summer
I saw a water snake caught between two locks

the canal
draining down
seeking the level

the snake
curving through the water
in a sudden tank

of gravity and engine oil
the fixed propeller
ticking over

the packet men threw coal
at the serpent
and shouted that it could go to hell

we balanced the beam
opening the green wooden gates

and the snake slithered
through the slough of rushes

back to the mid-element of fluvia
the adhesive edge of the world

Igloo

there was ice
on the inside of the windows

and snow
below the stairs

we were used to the cold
and expected the frost to bite

frozen pipes
girded the entire house
like the skeleton of a mammoth

we wore seven day socks
extra jumpers
hats

the lungs kept us warm
each breath melting and strengthening the bond

Red, White And Blue

dusty
with lint

geraniums wintered
in terracotta pots

if you brushed the leaves
you could taste

citrus
upon your fingers

the geraniums were colossal
like cacti

by the high days of summer
they flew the flag

of red, white and blue
in the proud clay of our frontage

the sun unsetting
swallows, shooting through the sky

the genteel punge of geraniums
spreading over the gardens of Middlesex

The Train to Devil's Bridge

though my mother swore
every day it rained

forward we went
on a wet day and the steam railway

toward clouds
the black eyed driver fed the red-hot stove

the old quarry train climbing
through forests and o'er rivers

the fork in the track
behind us

the train chugged into the station
my mother waving

at flies
her hair ruined

we spent the day
watching smoke rise and hiding from the devil

Expendable

parachutes shot to shreds
my soldiers dived
to a whirly death

on the patio
where my sister applied the coup de grace
with a magnifying glass

I watched them die
stretchy in the throes of their termination
and saw myself

thrown suddenly
from a window
by those I should trust the most

the expanding seconds of downfall
looping
through the plastic hoax of my life

my mother's scream from the window

Falling

my mother thought she was strong
well-armoured
against the outrageous cynicism of life

but dumbed by enemy action
my mother speaks
only when spoken to

maybe this moment
and then the next

are beautiful to her
in the curious light of her folly

something to hold onto
a stronghold of temperament

below
the hateful net tightens

My Mother's Dogs

when she falls
the whippet runs to a neighbour

when she leaves the gas on
the blood-hound howls

when she won't wake up
the labradoodle licks her face

she loves those dogs
and so do I

but when I visit
the beasts won't let me in

and gather around her
like children

when my mother dies
I will throw them sponge cakes

Morphine

she didn't recognise me

and I thought
why come?
stop this

there's no point in continuing

let her go
to that soft place

that breathes in the here and now
and does not think of tomorrow

but under the knife
she is deferred

held in the suspension of her room
by the thin tissue of her hand

I am
the hard determinate past

of microscopes
and second opinions

and like petals
that close at the end of the day

an intimation that mortality is definite

Fur

I am selling my mother's mink
(creeped)
at a furrier in St John's Wood

the fur exists
(as once did the mink)

maybe
an actor in a costume drama

will drape the stole upon her shoulders
and know her part

as did she
warming herself by one bar of the fire

the skin of the stars
twenty per cent of valuation

her acromatic monogram
undone

acromatic – a hybrid word from aromatic and acroamatic.

Echo
after John Gohorry

one brick upon another
we get up to all sorts of tricks

elaborate bonds
that rhyme a foot of clay

like a parabolic dish
words

are mortar
that hold the house together

even a whisper
that once heard as birdcall
I spoke back

Indigo Dreams Publishing
24 Forest Houses
Halwill
Beaworthy
Devon
EX21 5UU
www.indigodreams.co.uk